Death, Dying & Beyond

Practical information to guide you with stories and
experiences, providing insight into the process of
death, dying, grieving and the afterlife

Michelle Bourke

First published by Busybird Publishing 2020

Copyright © 2020 Michelle Bourke

ISBN

978-1-922465-35-1 (paperback)

978-1-922465-36-8 (ebook)

This work is copyright. Apart from any use permitted under the *Copyright Act 1968*, no part of this publication may be reproduced, stored in a retrieval system or transmitted in any form or by any means, electronic, mechanical, photocopying, recording or otherwise, without the prior written permission of Michelle Bourke.

Cover Image: Kev Howlett

Cover design: Busybird Publishing

Layout and typesetting: Busybird Publishing

Busybird Publishing
2/118 Para Road
Montmorency, Victoria
Australia 3094
www.busybird.com.au

*In loving memory of my husband Paul
and my mother Loryn,
who both lost their battles with cancer.*

Always Loved, Always Remembered

Contents

Section 1
Death 7

Section 2
Dying 37

Section 3
Beyond 65

Introduction

Hush, can you hear that? The word 'no' popped into my head.

Hush, can you see that? 'No' popped into my head again.

Hush, can you feel that? Yes, I could feel something, but I wasn't sure what it was.

I had just walked into the kitchen where Ollie, our dog, was barking at something in our back room and my daughter Sarah was frozen, saying, 'I'm not going in there, you have to.' I had faced this same scenario many times before, but this one was different because both Ollie and Sarah had a sense of something in the back room and didn't want to go anywhere near it.

My body started to tingle and buzz from head to toe, and the sensation became stronger as I moved closer into the darkened room.

I could sense something: a presence that I couldn't see physically but could feel energetically. As I spoke to whoever it was in the room, my body tingled and buzzed more. I spoke to this entity through thoughts, telepathy, as we conversed and introduced ourselves. The entity I was speaking to was a lost soul looking for their loved ones, who came across me thinking that I was the light that they were supposed to connect with. I told the lost soul that I wasn't their guardian angel or spiritual helper but could assist them in connecting with their own team of spiritual guidance. We chatted some more and then I asked them if they could see any bright lights around them. When they could, I told them that these were their guardian angels or spiritual helpers, and I told them to bring them in closer so they were touching them. Once we established connection, I asked the lost soul to go with their lights. I then cleansed and walked out of the room and told Sarah it was now safe to go into the back room.

Growing up Catholic, I believed in Jesus Christ and had a connection with Mother Mary, and I believed in reincarnation and knew that there must be something more than what was playing out on Planet Earth.

My grandmother was Catholic and very spiritual, and she also believed there was something else. She had a friend who would read coffee cups and tell the future. She loved to take me around to her friend's house for coffee. She wasn't aware that I had overheard a phone conversation that she had with her coffee-reading friend about me and what was happening in my life at that time. So, when it came time to have my coffee cup read, there was no surprise that the information my grandmother told her friend was the message read from my cup. I am sure my grandmother meant well, but I also believe she sat on the fence and didn't have a true understanding of spiritualism or of the unknown. Considering we were in the 1970s, the thought of following anything spiritual outside religion was not talked about or heard of. If anyone did work in the area, such as a clairvoyant, you only heard about them through word of mouth or recommendation and not in the mainstream, openly discussed as it is today.

Now, any kind of spiritualism is openly discussed and advertised, with physic fairs and spiritual expos being promoted and well attended. I find more people open to discussing all things 'new age', although it really is not new; it has been around since the beginning of time. History has shown us throughout the ages that people have sought guidance through the stars, mediums, rituals and witchcraft, to name a few. To know that most of us have lived through those previous lifetimes and reincarnated doing similar work in this lifetime is intriguing.

Since my grandmother passed on thirty years ago, I have had the fortune to connect with her and have the odd conversation. She used to visit me in my dreams, where we would be sitting somewhere and having a cup of tea and chatting. The dream felt real, so I know it was her. Another encounter I remember is standing at the clothesline, putting out the washing, when she came into my thoughts and I could smell the distinctive cigarette smell that always surrounded her. The conversation or thoughts were around her funeral and how many people attended and how proud she was of her grandson, who delivered her eulogy. She seemed lighter and free and was happy. We chatted for some time and then she vanished.

I haven't had a visit from my grandmother in a long time, but occasionally I will smell cigarette smoke, especially when I am visiting my mother, as my grandmother was inclined to hang around Mum more often.

I was in my late teens when all the weird things started happening to me that I couldn't really explain; I could only confirm that there was something else. I was seeing ghosts and apparitions at the end of my bed, and at one point my bed was shaking and I was being pulled to the top of my bed by something and it freaked me out. I thought there was an earthquake at one stage. But with all this weird stuff happening around me, I had this inner knowing and feeling that there was something more and I always followed my gut feelings. This was the beginning of my spiritual path and growth.

It wasn't until the 1990s, when I was in my thirties, that I started searching for the answers to my questions and why these things were happening to me. After experiencing and attending numerous spiritual modalities and workshops, it all fell into place when I was in my late forties. I finally had the answers I was seeking.

After moving through my fifties and losing the love of my life, I now have the true understanding of who I am and what my purpose is. It has taken nearly sixty years and many challenges, courage and heartache to realise my truth, my spiritual awareness.

This book is a practical guide for the dying process and ensuring everything is in place before we die. It is also about death and how I managed to prepare my beloved Paul for death and beyond. Plus, I get a little help from Paul along the way as I continue to talk with him after his death and receive the insights of what he has experienced since being in spirit. There are, of course, my experiences and stories throughout, plus stories of others that I have connected with and their experiences of losing a loved one and connecting from beyond the grave.

This is just an insight into my personal spiritual journey, with information gathered from knowledge, learnings and experience over forty-plus years. I hope that you will be able to relate, obtain some clarity and maybe get that lightbulb moment as I have.

Section 1

Death

Death is the finality of our reality.

Death definitions

> *The action or fact of dying or being killed; the end of the life of a person or organism.*
>
> – Lexico.com, Oxford University Press

> *Death is the permanent cessation of all biological functions that sustain a living organism. It is an inevitable process eventually occurring in all living organisms.*
>
> – Wikipedia

> *Death is the final outcome of the dying process.*

'I wonder what it is like on the other side. What if there is nothing there?'

This was a question that my late husband Paul asked in the last weeks of his life.

And I responded by saying, 'What if something is there? How amazing that would be, as we could continue to communicate with each other.'

Facing death is difficult because of what we are leaving behind, who we are leaving behind, and any doubts we may have about completing our own goals or purpose. There is also a fear of missing out.

Facing one's mortality is never easy and can be confronting. Accepting that you are going to die is courageous and brave but also brings peace of mind with the knowledge that everything and everyone left behind will be okay.

Watching your loved one battle illness is sad but also exhausting. The emotional turmoil of the rollercoaster ride is draining and challenging. When the loved one does die, there is a release of pain and anxiety, leading to an unexpected sense of freedom.

Death is such a taboo subject – not many people want to discuss death or dying. But if we are prepared and put all our affairs in place, including how we want our lives celebrated, it will make life so much easier for ourselves and the family when the time comes. Instead of talking about funeral arrangements, the person facing death can enjoy whatever time they have left without worrying about discussing their own death or adding more fear. It also assists family or friends experiencing the journey with them, and they can enjoy whatever time they have left together without concern for their loved one's final wishes.

Life is for living and loving and not worrying about dying.

The first ever experience I had with death was when I was a schoolgirl in the 1970s and being taught by the Sacred Heart nuns. We were often dragged to funerals of nuns who had died, with the usual ritual of saying the rosary and viewing the body before attending the funeral at the local church. This is where I viewed my first dead body as a teenager – an old nun that we didn't know was lying in her coffin in the convent and students were paraded past to view her body. At the time I didn't think much of it; it was just a body lying in a coffin. I didn't have any emotional attachment. Looking back on this experience, it could have been really confronting to some of the girls and I don't know what the nuns were thinking by putting us all through that ordeal.

When it came to personally losing a loved one, the first one was my grandfather, George, who died in 1988. He had a viewing too, at the local church. I decided not to see him, wanting to remember my beautiful grandfather as he was and not as just a body lying in a coffin. Maybe the earlier experience of seeing old nuns could have scarred me for life.

My grandmother, Leila, who I was extremely close to, died two years after her husband George. She also had a viewing of the body at the same local church. This time I decided that I wanted to see my beautiful grandmother, and as she laid there in her coffin peacefully, I thought she just looked the same but much older than she was.

We have choices about when and how we die and who is with us

When Leila became gravely ill and we knew she was dying, my husband Paul told me to go and see her. Leila lived in Alexandra, a country town in central Victoria, which was a two-hour drive from our house. Paul said, 'If you don't go and see her, you will forever regret not saying goodbye.' I made the two-hour drive that night and was able to spend some precious time before she passed away.

I was extremely grateful that I could spend those few days with her prior to her death as we talked and remembered certain moments in our relationship. She said she would love a cigarette, and even mimed the action of smoking. Leila also became very verbal and aggressive as she was going through the transition.

Leila held on for a few days prior to her death, waiting for her eldest daughter to visit her. My aunty and mother were both with her when she passed away and as I had driven back home by then, I received the phone call the next morning letting me know that she had died. I truly believe that my grandmother delayed her death, wanting to make peace with her daughter and ensure that she was surrounded by both her girls before she passed.

After experiencing the death of my husband Paul, and recently my mother Loryn, I came to the realisation that we really do choose when we die and who we want around us when we take that final breath. My grandmother's timing was not the best, as she died three days before my thirtieth birthday and we buried her on my actual birthday. Remembering exactly how long she has been gone is easy for me to recall.

Mum was terminal with metastatic breast cancer that had spread throughout her body and eventually to her lungs, causing pneumonia. I was fortunate to be able to be Mum's full-time carer over several months prior to her death.

When my mother was dying, she deteriorated over a week until she was put into a hospital bed at home in her lounge room. My sister Janine and I kept vigil, attending to her when she called out and ensuring she was comfortable and not in pain.

I had this strong feeling that Mum was going to die on the twenty-eighth of April, my wedding anniversary. But as that day passed, the next significant date was Mother's Day and although Mum was gravely ill, Janine and I were hoping that she would live for a few more days, as having to remember her anniversary as Mother's Day would be sad instead of a happy celebratory occasion. We were relieved when Mum hung on for another two days before dying.

Leading up to Mum's death, she slept during the day and was restless throughout the night, which didn't give us much rest and we became exhausted. It is extremely important that the family or carers look after themselves as well and don't burn out, as the dying process can take time. Mum took approximately ten days from the first signs of deterioration and difficulty breathing to death.

The night my mother passed away, we knew she was close to death and thought that she would pass sometime during the night. We planned an all-night vigil for my sister and I to sit with Mum. We had just finished our dinner; her husband Graham sat with her for a while, and then came out of the lounge where she was resting and my sister Janine took his place. Janine was sitting with Mum for about half an hour before she came out crying and distressed and said, 'Mum has stopped breathing.' We all rushed in and I placed my hand on her chest and her heartbeat was faint and then stopped. I checked the time and it was 6.54 pm. As we sat with her and cried, I was quietly thankful that Mum was now out of her pain and free again. She had chosen my sister Janine to be with her alone when she passed. Mum was seventeen days shy of her seventy-eighth birthday.

In life, I had a really close bond with Mum. In death, that bond was with my sister, Janine.

For years Mum was petrified of death, and didn't want to discuss it. In the few months leading up to her death, Mum seemed to be more comfortable with the idea and accepted that her time was coming to an end.

When my late husband, Paul, was towards the end of his life journey, I had this strong feeling that he would die on our wedding anniversary. On reflection, I realised that he had started to die on the twenty-eighth of April, our anniversary, as he was put on a morphine drive and said to me, 'Darling, this is the beginning of the end.' He chose to hang on for a further twenty days, as we were renewing our wedding vows after being married for twenty-five years.

Paul had been transitioning towards death for a few days, and on his final day he chose his family to be around him when he took his final breath. Paul passed away on a Friday afternoon at around 4.30 pm. We joked that this was typical

Paul – Friday afternoon at knock-off time, plenty of time to head home and relax for the weekend.

When I speak with others about the loss of their loved ones, they share similar stories of being witness to a loved one's death. It is quite common to hear that they have sat with a loved one on their deathbed, whether at home or hospital for weeks, days or hours, and have stepped out of the room for a break and returned to learn that their loved one has died. Some people decide that they want a crowd around them and some just want to be left alone.

I certainly believe that we choose the experience of how we want to die. It explains why you sometimes hear of tragic situations where people have perished in earthquakes, plane crashes or unforeseen circumstances and are unfortunately remembered for that event.

The process of dying, like birth, is completely different for each individual person. To witness someone's death or dying can be extremely confronting, emotional and sad, but it can also be rewarding and a privilege to be there for them in their final moment. Depending on the circumstances, it can also be devastating, particularly if the death was unexpected or tragic due to an accident, suicide or an unforeseen event.

Before Paul's cremation service, we had a viewing of his body. As he lay there peacefully, I stroked his hand and just noticed how old he looked – much older than his sixty-one years – and the bruising on his fingers as the body started to deteriorate.

We also had an open coffin viewing of Mum prior to the funeral at her home. Janine wanted to put memories of her family in the coffin, which included photos, some roses and her favourite rosary beads. Mum looked really awkward lying in her coffin. She had no makeup on and her hair didn't look great, so I grabbed her makeup and put some on and tried to fix her hair. But no matter what I did, it seemed to make her look worse and resemble the comic-book character the Joker. It was really funny but sad, as Mum always had makeup and lipstick on and was very stylish. I am sure she would have been looking down and shaking her head in astonishment.

Grieving

Those who have lost a loved one will be very familiar with grieving. Grieving is exhausting, energy zapping and sometimes overwhelming. We all grieve differently and at different stages; it's natural and human.

We are told that there are many stages of grief. From my experience, I don't necessarily agree with the step-by-step process of grief or the varying degrees we go through in our grieving and loss process. Grief and loss are very personal, physically and emotionally, and are different for each individual depending on their relationship with the deceased and how they died. Your actions and feelings may occur in different phases as you come to terms with your loss.

According to the experts, the different stages we go through in grief are denial, anger, bargaining, depression and acceptance. When faced with an anniversary, birthday or a familiar song, these reminders of loss may cause sadness or another feeling or emotion within.

I was heartbroken when my grandmother died and grieved her death for many years. I was so angry with her that she left when she did. Leila was still relatively young at seventy-three years of age, but battled ill health for many years and eventually succumbed to cancer.

With my grandfather, although I felt sad, the experience was completely different because I wasn't as close to him as I was to my grandmother.

Personally, for me, as I was losing the love of my life, Paul, and grieving his loss, we were fortunate to grieve together so that when he finally died, I was relieved and the pressure and weight on my shoulders was released. I could now relax and I felt free. This didn't mean that I was not saddened by his death – that came later in waves, and I was consumed by heartache as I came to terms with him being gone. At different moments, I felt like I was swimming in an ocean of emotions. One minute I would be fine and the next minute I would have waves of sadness; I would start to cry and then it was over in a few seconds. I couldn't control it. Just like ocean waves, these emotions hit me out of the blue. I found it difficult to manage the random waves of sadness.

I also had days when I felt extremely exhausted and my heart hurt. I could feel very flat and sad, and cry at the drop of a hat and ask a lot of questions, like 'why did you have to leave me so soon?'

It took me many months to actually talk about Paul's death without bursting into tears. It had been a long emotional journey and the majority of time I was on autopilot, so the relief afterwards was overwhelming.

Sometimes this feeling for me was very brief and sometimes it hung around for a few days. Physically, I got a migraine that wouldn't let up and I felt very tired and couldn't be bothered doing anything. My motivation was non-existent. I often went to bed late and would stay awake into the early hours of the morning, even as late as three am, because I just couldn't come to terms with sleeping without Paul.

But in the end, time was my healer. I accepted his loss and I honoured his memory in a very unique style, by travelling around the world with a cardboard cut-out of Paul in his wedding suit, which provided much comfort.

With Mum, I coped extremely well but as with Paul, I had already accepted her death and was grateful that I could spend those precious moments with her. I also knew, like Paul, that Mum was still around and I didn't really feel her loss – unlike my sister, who struggled with her death. My personal experience was to just let it happen and go with the flow, as I couldn't control it.

As we go through the grieving process, there is always help available and you can talk to someone about how you are feeling. For me, I didn't require counselling but had a good network surrounding me in my mother, children and friends. Grief counselling was offered to the family through the Palliative Care organisation and although I didn't use it, my son did, which helped him through his grieving journey.

I highly recommend that if you do need counselling, seek it sooner rather than later as this will assist you on your grieving journey. All I can suggest from my experience is that time is the healer. Although we never forget our loved ones, the feeling of loss becomes less and less as time goes by.

Recently, my daughter Sarah and I were talking about grief and trauma. She mentioned the symptoms of trauma and we both agreed that we had experienced similar feelings. We talked about her father and the experience she felt after his death. I know Sarah didn't want to talk about her father at all, so I didn't pursue any conversations and kept it light if he was mentioned. Sarah also became very upset and angry when I wanted to start cleaning out his clothes. Sarah explained that she retreated and became a different person for at least two years. I told her that I had to look at life in a positive way and move forward because if I dived into the black pool of emotions, I would never be able to surface again.

During the grieving process, be mindful of younger children and even young adults, as they may not understand what is happening and all they see is adults crying or being very sad.

When Paul was ill and dying, we were upfront with all of our children, even if they were late teens to young adults, and took them on the ride with us. They all had a say in having their father die at home, and at least they had that time to prepare for their grieving journey and to spend precious moments and create beautiful memories that we will all treasure.

Death is the finality of our reality

After Paul's death, I started attending meet-up groups to return to living some normality by meeting new people. At one particular meet-up group, a person I had just met came up to me and suggested that they could help me with my emotional grief. I advised them that I was fine and didn't require any treatment or assistance.

I see my grief now as being human. It is part of my uniqueness. It is acceptable for each of us to be sad and cry; it is a part of life. I believe that if I hadn't felt any emotion, then I would have sought help. My grief was manageable to me, but it may not be to others. Every single one of us is different and manages grief in different ways, at different stages and different times.

There are many people in specialist fields who know they can help others. However, it might be a good idea to step back first and ask the grieving person how they are doing and whether there is anything that you could help them with, instead of assuming that they need help and offering your services. We all mean well, but sometimes it's important to get the message across in a compassionate and empathetic manner without being insensitive.

I met a gorgeous woman who lost her husband the same year I lost mine. We started chatting about what we had done since our partners passed away. I told her how I had gone out and bought a new bedroom suite and car and started making my own decisions and how it had been an interesting experience. The woman mentioned that she didn't know what to do or what was expected of her as a grieving widow, considering that she wasn't an emotional person. There is no guide book on how to grieve, as we all grieve differently. I mentioned the waves of grief I felt and how I tended to cry privately.

This started me thinking about how other widows grieved, how they managed being alone all of a sudden. Since my own husband's death, it is amazing how many people I have met who have had similar experiences and have also lost their life partner. I'm not sure why; maybe it's the frequency I am now on.

Knowing that we are not alone and that we all go through similar journeys will help those experiencing the same.

After losing a loved one, some people find it difficult to talk to you as they don't know what to say. Many say, 'I am sorry for your loss', which I tend to find uncomfortable, but I know that this tends to be a common reaction when hearing of the loss. I am not sure why they feel sorry for the loss, as they had nothing to do with it. I like to rephrase the words and say something like, 'I am saddened by your loss', or, 'I am sad to hear that your husband, wife or partner (etc.) passed away'.

Death is considered by many to be too sad, too scary, too unfamiliar and therefore too difficult to discuss. Most people choose not to go there. They ignore death and dying until it slaps them in the face, until it's too late to prepare. Avoiding death only puts off the inevitable and leaves little time to be ready for what's ahead.

Preferring to focus only on life in an effort to somehow keep death at bay is a half-baked approach. Death is part of our lives whether we like it or not. Not talking about death is a missed opportunity, and many are compromised at the end of life because they chose to keep quiet.

COVID-19

Unfortunately, the global pandemic of COVID-19, or coronavirus, has challenged everyone, especially those directly affected and losing loved ones. It has also changed how we are treated when someone dies – we may not be able to be with our loved one when they pass, or the person dying is alone and not surrounded by family or friends.

I would also expect that the body of the deceased would be treated differently from a body that has died of other natural causes. According to the Department of Health, the bodies of people who have died from COVID-19 are required to be buried in a body bag within the casket and cannot be viewed at the funeral home.

The restrictions on people attending funerals have also caused major issues, as not all family or friends can attend in person and the decision about which close relatives to invite is difficult and heartbreaking. I was fortunate that Mum's funeral was organised a week after the initial stage-three restrictions ended, and we had the flexibility to invite more friends to her funeral which was held outside in her large garden.

Our uncle on Paul's side of the family died on the same day as Mum, but was less fortunate. His funeral was held indoors at a church in Queensland, and was limited to a certain number of attendees and live-streamed on Facebook.

Before we leave

As humans, all we want to know when we are on our deathbed is that our loved ones left behind are going to be okay, that we were loved and that we have permission to leave. In tragic or sudden circumstances, it is unrealistic to achieve this. For those who have a natural death, whether at home or in hospital, palliative care or hospice, there is the opportunity to spend time with loved ones and provide them with the comfort to know that everything will be okay and that they were loved.

When Paul was in his last hours of life, the four kids – Garry, Brendan, Matthew and Sarah – and I were keeping vigil, with someone always sitting with him. We all had an opportunity to say our personal goodbyes and let Paul know that he had our blessing to leave and that we would be fine.

The second youngest, Brendan, hadn't yet told his father that it was okay to go. So, Brendan sat quietly with Paul and said what he needed to say. Sarah and Brendan stayed in the bedroom with Paul and Ollie, our dog, on the bed. Within an hour of Brendan saying his farewell, Paul's breathing started to labour. Brendan called us all in and said this is it.

Brendan and Garry stood beside the bed, Sarah and Matthew were on the other side of the bed, and I sat at the end of our bed. I had this overwhelming feeling to say the rosary. Paul and I were brought up Catholic but were not practising. I had a pair of rosary beads that my grandmother gave to me in my side drawer. I pulled them out and proceeded to say the rosary. I was up to the last decade and I had this overwhelming emotional feeling of sadness and started to cry. By this time, Paul was breathing heavily and he would then stop. When he stopped, we would all cry out and tell him how much we loved him, and then he would start breathing again and we started to laugh. Paul made us laugh and cry until the very end. I had finished the rosary and felt like we needed music in the background, so I turned on the radio and had soft music playing. I moved to the top of the bed and as I held Paul's hand and stroked his forehead, which he loved, and kissed him, he took his last breath. We all cried and told him how much we loved him.

A few days before Mum died, I had the opportunity to speak with her. I told her how much I loved her and how I was forever grateful that she chose me for her daughter and that she was my mum. Janine had a similar discussion with Mum, as did my brother-in-law. We all gave permission for Mum to go in peace and to be out of pain. I asked her husband, Graham, if he had spent time with her, letting her know that it was okay to leave and that he would be okay, and he said that he hadn't. We left Graham to spend time with Mum to say his final farewells. Mum stayed around for another three days before she took her final breath.

Telling someone you dearly love that they have your blessing to leave can be extremely heartbreaking and is never easy. But for the person dying, it provides them comfort to know that they can leave without worrying about anything.

I had a conversation with Paul not long after his death about his experience and he offered this insight:

> *It wasn't easy to think about mortality, especially when you are leaving a life and family you loved with all your heart. It's the thought of leaving it all behind that's the hardest. Once the decision is made for you, you spend every second trying to hold onto life, trying to breathe and trying not to be in pain. The pain is overwhelming, not only physically but emotionally.*
>
> *I felt loss for weeks before I actually left because I knew I had to leave you behind. My 'life' now is peaceful and I don't have any pain. I only feel love and it is amazing.*

Lisa's story

Lisa is a beautiful lady who I met on the Britain and Ireland tour in 2017 and is also a widow. We connected on that trip and became friends. Lisa lives in Florida in the USA and we still keep in contact with each other. I asked Lisa to put some words together about her experience with her husband's cancer journey and loss. Here is Lisa's story.

Lisa met her next-door neighbour Tom in November 1975. They started dating and married in September 1977. Lisa knew that Tom's father had survived colon cancer and had a colostomy bag, but she didn't give it another thought.

In April 2000 they moved to a new townhouse with their thirteen-year-old son Ryan. In June of that year, Lisa noticed that Tom was losing weight and that their water bills had increased. It wasn't until a few months later, when Tom was feeling unwell, that the real story emerged. Lisa immediately took Tom to the doctor and after a series of tests, the results came back showing that his tumour marker carcinoembryonic antigen (CEA) was very high. Neither of them thought he could have cancer, let alone the same type as his father. They both cried.

Now the journey began. Lisa got Tom in to see a gastroenterologist for tests and then an oncologist. Strangely, he couldn't do anything because the tumour didn't indicate cancer. They had to get a surgeon to do a biopsy to confirm the cancer diagnosis before he could receive treatment. Meanwhile, he was painfully thin and sick.

They found a surgeon called Doctor Brilliant, who booked Tom in for a biopsy. The surgeon had to keep cutting away until the final diagnosis of a cancerous tumour was found. At this point they were thrilled that he could begin the treatment he needed. They operated on him to remove a rectal tumour and gave Tom a permanent colostomy bag.

They found some cancerous cells on his pelvic area but felt they had removed all of them. This was their new normal life, but at least he was alive.

Tom started chemotherapy and radiation sessions, and he was a trooper who never complained. Things started to get back to some resemblance of normalcy until mid-2002. They found cancer cells that had metastasised in his lungs and so Tom began an aggressive treatment. In June of that same year, Tom celebrated his sixtieth birthday with family and friends.

In March 2003, Tom went back into hospital with a bowel blockage caused by the scar tissue from the original surgery. He came home and seemed to be doing better. The specialist thought all was good until they found another rectal tumour in July of 2004. At this point nothing was curative, so Tom decided to go into hospice. The treatments had been brutal and his quality of life was poor and he thought, 'why prolong the inevitable'. He had given it his best shot. He just wanted to be comfortable and pain free.

Lisa and Tom made the decision to include their son, Ryan, from the age of thirteen. He would be aware of Tom's condition and included in the decision-making around Tom's illness. Both Tom and Lisa were very straightforward in conversations about death.

They decided as a family to have hospice come into their home for whatever amount of time Tom had left. They wanted him surrounded by family. He came home from hospital with a catheter and colostomy bag and never got out of the home hospital bed again. His mind was still sharp until the end.

Lisa made arrangements for Tom's cremation, and all she had to do was make a phone call to the funeral home for collection of his body when the time came.

Lisa continued working and had a palliative care, hospice and nursing team around the clock, supporting her and Ryan and caring for Tom.

During the last weekend of Tom's life, he had a seizure and went into a coma. Ryan and Lisa were at his side and held Tom's hands all weekend.

Lisa had scheduled a doctor's appointment for herself for the Monday, and when the hospice nurse arrived she asked whether there was time to run to the doctor. The nurse responded yes, go. Although Lisa knew that Tom's death was imminent, she didn't know when. While Lisa was leaving the doctor's office, she got the phone call from the nurse saying that Tom had passed away. Lisa was hysterical; she had been with him that whole weekend and he waited until she was not there.

Tom passed away on the twenty-third of February, 2005, at the age of sixty-two, leaving behind a fifty-three-year-old widow and eighteen-year-old son.

When Lisa thinks about Tom's death and her not being by his side, she believes that he did not want her there to see him die. Lisa recently spoke to Ryan to get his feedback on that time, and he thought it was interesting to see it from her perspective because he was young and says he mostly remembers the sadness.

It is extremely hard on kids. Ryan was only thirteen when his father became seriously ill. He supported Lisa during his illness and watched him die at the age of eighteen.

Lisa and Ryan went on a week's cruise to Alaska in June after Tom passed away. She realised it was far too soon to enjoy, even though she was with Ryan. Lisa wasn't emotionally ready.

After death: What do I do when someone has died? What are the next steps?

The next steps in relation to the body will depend on where the person has died. If it's in a hospital, palliative care or hospice, the staff will arrange to prepare the body and will ask the family to call the funeral director to collect the body. Staff will prepare paperwork so the doctor can sign off on the medical cause-of-death certificate, which will be handed over to the funeral director to allow the funeral arrangements to proceed.

If the death is at home, then there are many options available. The medical cause-of-death certificate has to be signed by a doctor but can be prepared by any other authorised person.

When Paul died at home, I immediately called our palliative care nurse, who attended our home to prepare Paul's body and complete the certificate. The nurse greeted Paul and talked to him with such respect for him and his body; it was really amazing to watch. We removed his clothes and bathed him with warm soapy water and changed him into a fresh black t-shirt and shorts, which had been the norm for so many months. The nurse removed the morphine drive and catheter; he was now free of all medical interventions. She also filled out all the forms confirming that Paul had passed away, as we needed this for the certificate. I gave all the heavy medication of morphine and sedation drugs to the nurse – I didn't want any of it in the house anymore. We laid Paul back on his pillow and placed a light blanket over him. He looked old and grey but peaceful.

When I arranged for the funeral director to come and collect Paul's body, I was able to provide the appropriate paperwork. The funeral director organised for the doctor's final sign-off within days of Paul's death.

Prior to Mum passing away, I was provided instructions from our lovely palliative care nurse to contact the emergency services when Mum died, as the local doctor would not be available after hours to attend the home to sign the medical cause-of-death certificate.

After Mum died, I dialled the emergency number and had the lights and sirens of the local fire brigade turn up at our door. I walked out to greet them and advised them that I was instructed to contact them because Mum had passed away. They offered their condolences and contacted the paramedics and police to attend the house. Within half an hour, the paramedics arrived and proceeded into the lounge room where Mum was resting. They performed an ECG to confirm that her heart had stopped beating and she was confirmed deceased. Whilst the paramedics were packing up their equipment, the policewoman arrived to complete her report. The certificate was completed and ready to be handed to the local doctor for signature the following morning.

Mum was kept overnight, as it was too late for the funeral director to come and collect her body. The following day the palliative care nurse arrived to prepare her body. The nurse and I washed Mum's body and changed her clothes. We spoke to Mum gently and with respect. Mum had some jewellery on her that I wanted to remove. I grabbed some body oil and rubbed this into her fingers to loosen up the rings that were tight on her hands. We eventually removed her rings and two bracelets from her wrists. I contacted the funeral director and he arrived later that afternoon to collect her body. I had the outfit that she was going to be buried in ready for him to take. When the funeral director arrived, my brother-in-law and I helped the funeral director transfer Mum from the hospital bed onto the gurney.

The medical cause-of-death certificate contains details about the person who has died and the funeral location, and is provided to the Registry of Births, Deaths and Marriages so that the death can be officially registered. The final death certificate is not available until all of this information has been submitted. The death certificate is mailed to the executors or family representative within a period of time to finalise the estate.

Celebrating

When our loved one has died, there is an opportunity to celebrate their life. Although funerals can be extremely sad, it is a chance for family and friends to gather and honour and remember that person's life.

Each funeral is very personal and although very emotional, it can be an amazing experience to express love for the person who has died. Pre-arranging your funeral will provide your family with direction as to how you want to be celebrated and whether you want to be buried or cremated.

Organising a funeral can be simple if you know what your loved one wanted or they had a pre-arranged funeral plan in place. Otherwise, funerals can be a big job as it involves organising an event and ensuring that everyone is invited and you have all the pieces in place.

Paul was very particular with what he wanted, and we had his piece of paper with all the instructions ready. Paul wanted two ceremonies, one at the church and one at the crematorium. We chose a simple coffin and red and white roses. Paul didn't want bells and whistles. He wanted something simple but nice and wanted it all on a small budget, not too expensive. In preparing the content for the services, I found some great websites that helped with readings for the church service.

During all this preparation, the funeral directors told me four days prior to his funeral that we needed to organise our own priest for the church service. There was a huge sense of panic trying to work out who we would get as our priest. I contacted Paul's eldest brother, David, who said to leave it up to him, he would find someone. Within a few hours we had a priest and a time scheduled for us to meet with him. The priest came over and the kids and I sat around and prepared for the funeral service. It was helpful as the priest was able to provide templates and guidelines.

I prepared the funeral booklet with readings and music to accompany the celebration. Putting the funeral booklet together and having it printed on time was stressful and costly.

As I had organised Paul's funeral, I knew what to expect with Mum's funeral, so I was fully prepared and organised. I had contacted the funeral director a few days prior to Mum's death. It was beneficial to have that first contact to discuss what was happening, and they were ready when I called for them to collect Mums' body. We chose a simple white coffin for Mum and organised her favourite flowers, roses and hydrangeas, to be placed on top.

As I knew Mum's death was not too far away, I started putting together the funeral preparations, including the eulogy, music and prayers. I had chatted with Mum a few weeks before her death and asked her what her favourite songs were and what she wanted played at her funeral. This made my job easier when it came time to include those songs in her celebration.

Because there were strict COVID-19 restrictions in place, Mum's funeral was at home in her back garden so that we could accommodate the maximum number of people allowed to attend.

You can choose to arrange the funeral by yourselves and call upon the funeral director for the fundamentals, or you can hand everything over to the funeral directors and they will organise everything for you. It just depends on your budget and how much time you want to spend preparing for the event.

I highly recommend that a discussion around death and what you want is had well before the time comes. Having the funeral organised and prepared with a list of all requirements helps the family or those organising the event, especially when they are grieving.

At the end of the day, you have complete control over how you want to die and where. If each and every one prepares for their death and dying the way they want, then you will have your death journey on your terms, and family and friends need to accept and honour your wishes.

Dying

Dying definitions:

On the point of death.

Gradually ceasing to exist or function; in decline and about to disappear.

– Lexico.com, Oxford University Press

Dying is the process of the body ceasing to function, where the final outcome is death.

'I wonder what it is like on the other side. What if there is nothing there?'

As humans, we go through life believing we will live to a ripe old age and probably die in our sleep, and we will worry about that stuff when it happens. Unfortunately, this thinking is not realistic.

Just imagine your worst nightmare: you find a rash or lump somewhere on your body and go to the local doctor to have it checked. Before you know it, you are being sent off for a series of tests and biopsies and referrals to specialists. Then specialists start talking about diagnosis, treatments and results and the next steps. Your life starts to unravel and becomes a never-ending rollercoaster of decisions, emotions, anxiety and worry.

This nightmare began for our family in 2008 when my late husband Paul found a rash on the side of his neck, and within a few days he was at the Peter MacCallum Cancer Centre having surgery to remove the rash. He was diagnosed with skin cancer, melanoma. Once the surgery was completed and he had recovered, we didn't give it another thought and life continued, although he had to see the oncologist every three months for a check-up.

Fast-forward six years and the nightmare returned. The melanoma recurred, but this time in his spine. It took three months to find the real cause of his symptoms due to misdiagnosis and believing it was another issue that was causing his paralysis. When he was finally admitted to hospital for an MRI, the scan revealed a tumour sitting in his spine, in the thoracic area. Within twenty-four hours he was having spinal surgery, as the tumour was putting pressure on his spine and the concern was that it could permanently paralyse him. After the surgery, the results came back from the tumour removal and although we were not quite sure what it was, on Christmas Eve in 2014 we were told that the melanoma had returned. But it was not your everyday melanoma; no, it was a rare form called 'KIT'.

From that day, Paul endured a further four spinal surgeries and one brain surgery plus radiation, immune therapy and weeks of rehabilitation over a twelve-month period. During this time we had many close calls, and believed that he could die after any one of the surgeries, especially the brain one, as he had a brain bleed and could have gone into a coma at any moment. We lost months and months of normal life, surrounded by oncology appointments, blood tests, PET scans, radiation sessions, MRIs, CAT scans and everything else that is thrown at you when you go through the cancer journey.

We knew that this melanoma was serious and deadly, but we always had hope that a miracle would occur.

I broached the subject of preparing for death to Paul whilst he was in hospital recovering from the fourth spinal surgery, after complications of a spinal leak that put him back in the critical life-and-death situation. Paul and I talked about dying and what he wanted, but he didn't want to talk about it that much. Maybe because he couldn't think about life after death, not living anymore without me or the kids.

I left a notebook in the side drawer beside his hospital bed and said if you don't want to discuss it, then write it down. The book remained blank and no discussion was had, although we had already arranged for our wills to be created after the first spinal surgery.

It wasn't until the week before he died and the last oncology appointment at Peter MacCallum, where his oncologist told us that there was nothing more they could do, that he started to plan.

After arriving home, Paul sat on the computer and started shopping around for coffins. He also grabbed a scrap piece of paper and wrote down what he wanted. We spoke of him having two ceremonies and he was still deciding whether he wanted to be buried or cremated. I have always spoken about and planned for cremation, with my ashes spread over the Alexandra hills in central Victoria. I said to Paul that you can still be buried and when I am gone, the kids can put my ashes in with you. He said, 'No, I will be cremated because I just want to be with you.' He was ever the romantic, even in death.

Although Paul delayed talking about his funeral arrangements, along his cancer journey we continually discussed his treatment and where he wanted to die, whether it be in hospital or at home. We both chose home, as we had had enough of hospitals, plus it was very cold and clinical to be living your last days in a hospital. We were very fortunate that palliative care had already been arranged and was supporting us in conjunction with the Royal District Nursing Service for Paul's care at home. Along the way we didn't have an advanced care plan, as this was just starting to be rolled out through the health system, but I had a clear understanding of what Paul wanted care-wise in those last weeks. He wanted to die with dignity and as far as I could possibly arrange that, he did die with some dignity.

Through our cherished loved ones we get to end our lives in dignity. Those who take on this important role in our end-of-life plan, transitioning us along the dying journey with such love, peace and harmony, is all we could ever hope for.

Where to start?

It is extremely important to have a legal will in place to ensure that assets are distributed in the way you want. I highly recommend that a will is made sooner than later. You don't have to wait until a terminal illness diagnosis, because you just don't know when the end is near.

If someone dies without a will, they die intestate. Intestate means that the laws of the state or territory they lived in will decide how their estate is administered. Depending on your state or territory within Australia, the names of these roles or documents may differ.

Important documents include:

- **standard legal will**
- **enduring power of attorney**
- **appointment of medical treatment decision-maker**
- **advance care directive or plan**
- **statement of wishes.**

A will is a legal document that allows you to decide how your 'estate' is to be distributed after your death. This includes money, property, shares, investments and possessions. Instead of leaving it to others or to chance, you decide how you want your assets to be distributed.

A suggestion is to choose your executors wisely, and make sure that they have the capacity to follow your wishes and ensure that everything is divided evenly and fairly.

It is extremely important to ensure you have an updated will, especially if there are any changes to your circumstances, such as marriage, divorce, etc.

If you want to give any particular items to loved ones, including money, that are not included in your will, these treasured belongings can be itemised in a separate document to your will. This statement of wishes is not binding but can assist your executors when it comes time to administering your estate. This document can be stored with your will.

Just ensure that you have everything in place and all wishes and gifting accounted for, because once you die, the executors or family have to sort out the estate and it can be extremely emotional, as they have lost a loved one.

When it comes to handling inheritance, estates and money, it can be amicable or, unfortunately, very nasty, where greed takes over and people can even become vindictive. Over the years, I have heard horror stories of families fighting over inheritance to the point where the family has been divided and relatives no longer speak.

An enduring power of attorney is a legal document that allows you to nominate one or more persons (referred to as an attorney or attorneys) to act on your behalf for legal, financial and personal decisions. This document is extremely important, especially if you lose the ability to make your own decisions. It is very wise that you choose the right person that you can trust and has your best interests at heart and is able to make the correct decisions when the time comes.

A medical treatment decision-maker is someone you can choose to make your medical decisions for you. This document used to be called a medical enduring power of attorney, but this terminology has changed in recent years.

In the past decade, a document called an advance care plan was introduced to ensure there is a formal process for conversations to occur in relation to clarifying people's wishes, needs and preferences and deliver care to meet these needs.

The advance care plan provides:

- **an instructional directive with legally binding instructions about future treatment the person consents to or refuses**

- **a values directive which documents the person's values and preferences for future medical treatment.**

Whether or not you have been diagnosed with a terminal illness, it is highly recommended that you have an advance care plan completed sooner rather than later. Having an advance care plan in place will ensure that the final weeks will be calmer and you can concentrate on spending precious time with loved ones.

Also, put plans in place for how you want to spend your last weeks and days, whether it be at home or in palliative care, hospice or hospital. Unfortunately, in some situations you may not have a choice, depending on the circumstances, and your requests may be taken out of your hands. Personally, staying at home until the very end surrounded by loving friends and family would be my choice.

I highly recommend putting plans in place well before the time comes, before it is too late.

Terminal illness journey

When Paul was going through his cancer journey, I found along the way that I had to learn quickly about what to do and how to manage what we were facing. I found that I wasn't being supported effectively or comprehensively through the health system. We were fortunate to have some information provided, but we didn't have a one-stop shop or avenue to understand the bigger picture of what was actually going on or where it would end. We also had conflicting information, depending on the specialist or hospital. This lack of support or knowledge just led to confusion, anxiety and frustration, which you really don't need when a loved one is terminally ill.

Based on my experience, I would like to make some suggestions to assist those who are beginning or are already in the health system, which just might help. It is easier to provide the appropriate care when clear instructions are discussed well ahead of time.

Advocate

I highly recommend that, if someone is seriously ill or terminal, they have an advocate at all times when visiting specialists and going for treatment. Unfortunately, the one going through the treatment will not be focused on certain points about their health or treatment due to trying to survive. Some may go into survival mode, some into shock or denial, plus there are side effects from the treatment, which can cause exhaustion, fogginess of the brain, confusion and many other symptoms. Have someone on your side you can trust to be your advocate and support person. Usually, this advocate will be a close loved one or relative.

I also suggest that the carer or advocate write down any questions that require answering, and keep notes. Throughout the journey, you will often be overloaded with medical jargon and may not have a clear mind; it just helps to write questions down and keep notes to refer to at a later date.

Medications

Keep a list of all drugs and medications on you each time you visit a doctor or specialist or hospital. You will be asked about this constantly and if you have the list, you won't be racking your brain trying to think of what you or your loved one are taking. During the time of illness, especially if terminal, you are bombarded with so much information that it can be difficult to remember everything or anything.

Your local chemist that dispenses your medication can provide you with this list, so it is much easier to hand over a piece of paper.

Forms

I found it extremely frustrating that every time Paul was admitted to the same hospital for surgery, he was asked to complete volumes of forms. Honestly, there has to be a better way, considering we are in the age of technology. You would think that if the patient is returning to the same hospital, they would have current information available online. Since I haven't been in the hospital system for over five years, the procedures may have changed. I certainly hope they have.

Paul had five admissions to the same hospital in a twelve-month period and we had to complete new admission forms every time. After the second admission, I took a copy of the original admission form document and then had it on hand every time we had to complete this form again. At least all the information was up to date and we didn't have to remember every single detail as it was all there (although I still had to fill out the form by hand).

To have to complete forms in this situation only adds frustration and distress to all involved. Plus, the patient requiring care is not well or not thinking straight, and is anxious prior to any admittance or surgery!

Superannuation and life insurance

It is a good idea to ensure that your superannuation (if applicable) and life insurance are up to date and beneficiaries are current. When Paul was first diagnosed as terminal, we started to put our affairs in place by arranging a legal will and sorting out his superannuation. Paul had at least five different superannuation schemes with different organisations. I contacted our financial consultant who assisted in minimising Paul's superannuation into two policies that had death and disability insurance linked to them. This made it so much easier to access after his death.

Some people may have life insurance policies separate from their superannuation. It helps if you are aware of the different policies and are able to place the documents when the time comes.

Do we really plan to celebrate our lives?

After Paul's death I spoke to many people, and often during the conversation they would mention that when their loved one was dying, they did not discuss funeral arrangements or what they wanted, so the family was left to guess what they would have liked.

I find it hard to believe that talking about death is such a taboo subject. Why can't we talk about death and how we want to celebrate our lives?

We don't really know how to talk about death in general. We don't want to discuss any funeral celebrations or how we want to be remembered, and we usually leave it up to our loved ones to organise. Some find the death topic too emotional or distressing or even macabre. I find this really difficult to understand, as we all know for a fact that we die at some time, so why wouldn't we want to discuss it?

Dealing with a loved one who has died is very confronting to say the least, no matter if it is sudden, terminal or a natural death. The majority of us don't have skills or training in preparing a loved one for death. As it is a very emotional time for loved ones, the thought of planning and organising can be very overwhelming and daunting.

Why let your family go through unnecessary drama and grief when you can simplify that for them now? Don't be that burden. Let the family be in a position to celebrate and honour you and the life you lived the way you want to; it is your journey. You have control, the last say.

It's never too early to plan.

We all plan for birth, marriage, birthdays and weddings but most of us don't plan our funerals. These are major events that we meticulously and perfectly plan and invite all our family and friends to. We think of every detail and experience we want to have in that celebration, in that moment. Remember that when organising a funeral, you only have a short window of opportunity to prepare and plan this final celebration. Funerals are usually put together within a week or two at the most. It doesn't make sense to put this pressure on your loved ones during an extremely emotional time.

The only difference between planning a major celebration and a funeral is that we don't have a date.

Some things to consider to relieve the burden on loved ones when the time arrives:

- **Have a personalised end-of-life plan**
- **Have knowledge and insight about what to expect**
- **Plan milestones**
- **Have your funeral planned**
- **Assist your loved ones by stating your final wishes**
- **Replace feelings of confusion and overwhelm with clear direction and focus**
- **Transform your lifetime gains into meaning and purpose**
- **Celebrate how you want to be celebrated**
- **Have the final say!**

There is plentiful information available that discusses death and dying and preparing for death. There are also many support services that you can contact when the time comes.

Palliative Care

Palliative Care is an amazing service provider and resource to connect with. It assists the patient and their families through the prevention and relief of suffering and improving the patient's quality of life. They will work with you to provide a treatment plan, medication when needed and equipment, including hospital beds.

They are such a remarkable group of caring people that support the family and I couldn't have survived without their support during Paul's final journey. After his death, the palliative care nurse came to prepare Paul's body and the paperwork. They also provided grief counselling to the family.

Death doula

A death doula is a non-medical role providing support, comfort and information to assist the dying and those around them. They provide knowledge, assistance and support during times of uncertainty.

During Paul's illness and dying at home, I would have loved to have known about death doulas and would have embraced the support. Caring for a loved one alone with minimal support is trying and exhausting, and I certainly would have welcomed the additional support if I was aware of their services.

Let's talk about death

Death is a very interesting subject to discuss, although some may not agree. Whether the discussion is around planning for one's death or after a loved one has passed away, the subject can be rather awkward and people just don't know what to say, how to say it or when.

How do you start a conversation about death and dying?

As Mum was a practising Catholic, I knew she wanted to be buried and I had a fair idea of the service she would want, but had no idea about the music. In the last few weeks, we would sit together on her veranda just chatting, and I started to talk about songs she loved and played some tunes on my phone. I asked what songs she would like at her funeral and as I played a song, she would say 'I love that song'. Mum had mentioned to her niece that the song she wanted played whilst her coffin was being lowered was 'Goodnight Sweetheart' written by Al Bowlly in 1931, well before Mum's birth.

Personally, I have never had an issue with talking about death and have spoken on many occasions of how I want to be cremated and where I wanted my ashes to be spread. I am not really sure why I am so comfortable with talking about death. Maybe I am a realist and know that one day my time will come, and I want to ensure that I don't leave it up to my children to make decisions on my behalf, organising my last major celebration or event. I want the last say!

Broaching the subject of death with any family member can be a bit tricky, and if you know them well, you will be able to drop the subject into a conversation and keep it light – you don't have to go all morbid. Maybe start with a conversation around what you want to achieve before you die, your dreams and wishes and the bucket list, and then take it from there.

What do you say when someone has died?

I have found that people will support you for a short period of time and then you won't hear from them again, or for months afterwards. Family do the same, especially in-laws, once the family member has passed on. It depends on the relationship you had together when the family member was alive, but it will often be totally different once they have passed on.

For those loved ones who find it difficult to discuss their end-of-life wishes, I have developed simple forms and guidelines that can be filled out and placed with their wills and important documents. These forms can also be an opportunity to open up a discussion about death and dying with your family.

Let's do some planning …

If you have organised events such as birthdays, births, marriages and engagements, why would you leave the most important and last event, celebrating your life, to someone else? Why not have the last say!

Don't leave it to the last minute. Be prepared, because your loved ones may not be.

Death is a celebration of one's life and it is important to have your input into honouring your achievements and celebrating the life you shared.

This table is a simple way of writing down your wishes if you are unable to discuss death or dying with loved ones.

Statement	Yes	No	Comments
Have you got an updated will?			
Have you got an advance care plan?			
Have you nominated an enduring power of attorney?			
Have you got an insurance policy that covers death?			
Has your superannuation been finalised and a beneficiary nominated?			
Are you an organ donor?			
Do you want to be resuscitated?			

If you do not want to be resuscitated, have you completed the 'do not resuscitate' document?			
Have you arranged a pre-paid funeral?			

This is an opportunity to think about and plan for what you really want at your own funeral.

Organising the funeral

Statement	Yes	No	Comments
Preferred funeral director			
Religion			
Burial			
Cremation			
Church service			
Memorial service			
Family viewing			
Flowers			

Donations in lieu of flowers			
Charity/organisation for donations			
Something of meaning			
Photos			
Audio-visual presentation (DVD)			
Favourite songs			
Favourite poems			
Favourite prayers			
Favourite outfit			
Item to be buried with (e.g. ring)			
Coffin			
Cars			
Place where ashes are to be spread (in the case of cremation)			

After your loved one has passed, their estate needs to be sorted and documentation finalised.

There are a number of people and organisations that may need to be contacted when someone passes away. This checklist is a helpful guide that can assist the family in finalising the deceased person's affairs.

The majority of documentation cannot be finalised until receipt of the death certificate.

Sorting out the estate

Statement	Yes	No	Comments
Contact solicitor (will)			
Accident insurance			
Accountant			
Age pension enquiries			
Ambulance services			
Australian Tax Office			
Bank/s			
Centrelink			

Drivers licence cancellation			
Medicare			
Electricity			
Gas			
Water			
Local council			
Vehicle registration			
Health insurance			
Vehicle insurance			
Home insurance			
Superannuation organisation/s			
Phone company			
Mobile phone company			
Internet provider			

Some other things to keep in mind

Statement	Yes	No	Comments
EBay account			
Passwords			
Email account			
Facebook			
Other social media			

Are you ready to start having a conversation around death and dying?

It is never too early to start planning your final celebration and talking about death or dying.

Some ideas to start the conversation:

- **List at least seven things you need to do before you die.**
- **List your meaningful milestones that you want to achieve.**
- What is the most important value to you?
- What is it that you cherish most?

- **List at least seven things you want to achieve before you die.**

- **Have you started a wish list? Have you checked anything off your to-do list?**

I can assure you that I am not leaving anything to chance and am ensuring that I am well prepared before my end date arrives.

Continue to live life to the fullest and create memories because as we know, life is far too short.

Section 3

Beyond

The veil between this life and the next is very thin.

I am in your past

I am in your future

But I am not in your now

'I wonder what it is like on the other side. What if there is nothing there?'

This was a question that my late husband Paul asked in the last weeks of his life.

And I responded by saying, 'What if something is there? How amazing that would be, as we could continue to communicate with each other.'

When Paul asked this question, I had a fair idea of what the other side was like.

My conversations with Paul from beyond confirmed my initial idea of the other side and provided a clearer understanding of what the picture was from his point of view.

As humans, we have our own opinions and perceptions of life and death. I am not here to persuade or prove to anyone what they should or shouldn't believe. This is my experience based on information that I have channelled from those who have more insight than I do – information from ascended masters, archangels and my own team of spiritual guidance, who have lived multiple lifetimes and certainly have inner knowledge and experience.

This section, Beyond, provides information and insight for those seeking to obtain some clarity and assistance as they travel on their own personal spiritual journey.

What happens after we die?

We are each a soul in a body experiencing life and learning lessons as we navigate our way through multiple lifetimes. Our soul is unique, pure energy, and captures all memories and feelings experienced in all those lifetimes. The soul is endlessly evolving and moving forward.

As souls, we have the same perceptions and although we have free choice, what we believe to be our heaven or home of the afterlife will be based on that internal belief or perception. When the body dies and the soul's purpose and contract has expired, the soul leaves the body and returns home with help from guidance or a loved one.

Do we really lose someone when they die? I have thought about this question for some time and don't believe so. We are all energy and although physically here in body, when we die, our life essence still remains in the hearts and memories of those loved ones left behind and we are still connected.

On the day my husband Paul passed away, I was ready and prepared as my guidance had already informed me that Paul was leaving his body and returning home. On that day, in the early hours of the morning, Paul whispered his last words to me. 'I am sorry for putting you through all this.'

I said, 'That is okay, darling, this is what we chose to do together. I love you for eternity.'

It had been a crazy couple of days and Paul was now quiet and heavily sedated. His breathing became heavy and he could no longer swallow.

I sat beside his bed and said, 'It won't be long, my love, just rest.' I looked at the clock and it was around 10.30 am; I had the thought that by 7.30 pm that evening, he would have left us. I looked up at the top of his bed and saw his Aunty Shirley standing there. Shirley had left us many years before, succumbing to the horrible motor neurone disease. I felt so much love and comfort and was happy that his beloved aunty would be there for Paul when he left us.

Janine, my sister, who had been staying with me for a few days, came out into the kitchen and said she had a terrible feeling that Paul was going to die that day. I said to her, 'Yes I know, it is just when.' Janine was packed up ready to head home and asked me if I wanted her to stay. I said, 'No, you need to get home to your family ... we will be fine. I will let you know of any updates.'

I walked Janine out to her car and gave her a big hug. I told her that I had this overwhelming feeling of peace and freedom and felt really excited. Why I would feel that is beyond me as I was losing my soul mate, my true love, within the next few hours. By now I was so tuned and connected to Paul, this may have been what he was feeling. I hope it was, as it was an amazing feeling. It might also be that I had finally come to the end; I was exhausted and wanted this freedom for such a long time, and now it was within my grasp. I didn't want my beautiful Paul to leave – only the cancer.

That whole day, although the weather outside was warm, the house was freezing cold. I joked to Garry, our son, that the spirits were circling, preparing Paul. It was very eerie and we both got the tingles and shivers.

Janine rang me mid-afternoon and said she had been driving through Elmore in Victoria and the feeling she'd had that morning of Paul dying was only getting stronger. I again said I knew, but it was all about when.

Paul has recently told me that when I was saying goodbye to Janine out the front of our house just before he passed away, he was moving in and out of his body, transitioning between this life and the next. He was floating around ensuring that everyone was going to be okay and witnessing his own death. He was disconnected from the body, but his soul returned so he could be there when he took his last breath. He wanted to be present to experience what it was like to actually die and for the soul to leave the human body. No wonder I felt so peaceful and free that morning.

Afterlife: What is it like?

The afterlife has a different perspective for every single soul. What you might believe or visualise as a human is totally different to what the afterlife is actually like. What my ideal vision of home or heaven is like will be totally different to someone who has a strong religious background. The afterlife is whatever your soul wants it to be.

From all the trance medium work I have done over the years, I always feel calm and at peace, even though I tend to pick up on the memories and feelings of souls at the time of connection. I have had some souls come in for healing feeling confused or trapped and, depending on how they died, they also may not realise they have died or are dead. I find that once the soul has connected with their guidance, the feeling of release and calmness is instant and I certainly feel it in my body. It is actually an honour to be able to do this work and assist souls to connect with loved ones or be able to transition home.

Whenever I visit the other side in trance, I always feel at peace and calm and see white light. I remember, years ago, I did a meditation and was asked to return home. I could see a large beautiful tree with lush green grass and a rainbow in the distance. It felt like home and free with no worries or concerns; it was a beautiful feeling.

Appearances of spirits and ghosts

Have you seen something out the corner of your eye, a shadow? Have you sensed something, but cannot see anything? Have you felt a chill in the air or cold patches in certain places that you cannot explain?

It was explained to me that those who see apparitions or ghosts are actually seeing the soul as energy. When they appear, it is because they can expand their energy in or out, being compact or expansive. Seeing an apparition or ghost is the soul expanding its energy out so you can see a shadow, be it dark or light. It is like our aura energy field around the human body. They take on a similar format as to how they looked in that lifetime or how you remembered them. For a soul to do this, it takes a considerable amount of energy, hence why you may only see them for a fleeting moment.

Our loved ones can also communicate through thoughts or sounds. When Mum passed away and all the emergency services had left, I walked out into the front yard and looked up at the night sky and stared into the dark with stars shining brightly and said, 'Hi Mum, how are you?' And all I heard or thought in my head was the Michael Bublé version of the song 'Feeling Good'. When I heard the words to the song, at that moment I knew Mum was and would be alright.

Our loved ones will often visit, and sometimes we can sense them and other times we cannot; it just depends on how you are feeling at the time. The more relaxed you feel, the more you will tune in to them.

Cleansing

Each of our bodies is surrounded by an energy field or aura, which is our ethereal body. The ethereal body changes and will change consistently, depending on our environment, emotions and people that surround us. Our ethereal body is always changing, evolving, lifting and vibrating.

There are many ways to keep your aura and spiritual space cleansed. It is important when doing any work in the spiritual area that you remain cleansed regularly to ensure that you keep your vibration high. There are many techniques available including smudging your environment, burning incense or imagining white light surrounding you.

I have a particular technique that I learnt more than ten years ago and use multiple times throughout the day. The more I remain cleansed, the more I am calm and have direct contact with my spiritual guidance.

Communicating with those from beyond

I have been very fortunate to be able to communicate with the souls of loved ones that have returned home and my own personal team of spiritual guidance.

Every one of us has this ability to communicate with our loved ones, which is in the form of our four different types of communication. The only tricky bit is how we do this, but the majority of us do it automatically without even knowing.

The four forms of communication are:

- **Intuition**
- **Visionary**
- **Prophetic**
- **Feeling**

Intuition is using the psychic form of clairaudience, or clear hearing. This can come through messages from loved ones as words, memories, sounds or music. After Paul passed away, I would often hear our song played on the radio or be taken back to something that we had done via a memory.

Vision is using the psychic form of clairvoyance, or clear seeing. These messages come through pictures and images in the mind. Paul would often send me images of when he was in hospital and I would often say to him, 'Why are you sending me those memories?' I didn't want to go back there and remember those dark days.

Prophecy is using the psychic form of trance, or an inner knowing. I use this gift to connect with loved ones, which is similar to daydreaming. I also use this psychic form of trance, called trance healing, when souls come through for healing.

Feeling is being very aware and sensitive of your true feelings. This is similar to getting a gut feeling or all of a sudden feeling sad or happy, knowing that it is not your true feeling. I find that I am very sensitive to energy changes and can feel very excited or emotional for no apparent reason.

With all these forms of connection and communication, we can move in or out of any one of them at any time. One of these types of communication will tend to be stronger or predominate the others.

In one of the conversations I had with Paul from beyond, he provided me with a visual of how we communicate telepathically. He showed me an old switchboard plug and cord that operators used a long time ago and explained that plugging into the switchboard (soul) from beyond into the human provided a connection through thoughts. With my four different types of communication, my connection with Paul is through mediumship or trance, which is utilising my prophetic gift; I have thoughts or words that come to mind, which is using my intuitive gift; flashes of places or memories are my visual gift and I will always have an emotional reaction, which is my feelings gift coming into play.

Divine timing

Everything we do is not by chance; it is always in divine timing. No matter how much we want something it will not come to us until the right time. And in universal timing, there is no timing as this is a man-made, human concept.

I have often manifested jobs and always found that the right job at the right place at the right time will arrive when

I am ready – no sooner, no later. With the last job I applied for, I had been looking for work and nothing was available or suitable. Months later, a thought popped into my head and I looked up jobs and there appeared a job that was not only suitable for my skill set but in a perfect location, and everything flowed easily and effortlessly.

If we are impatient and trying to obtain something that is not right for us or has the wrong timing, we will be faced with obstacles or roadblocks and nothing flows. But when it is right, everything will fall into place perfectly.

This concept covers all areas of life: jobs, love, travel, home, etc. If we are searching for something and obstacles arise, then the timing is off. If everything flows easily and just happens to appear, then it is divine timing.

Dreams

Our loved ones who have passed often visit us in our dreams and although we may dismiss this, it is a vehicle for those who have died to be able to return and visit those left behind. The dreams tend to occur not long after the loved one has passed, but with time, these dreams can become fewer and fewer.

After Paul died, I often dreamt about him, especially in the weeks straight after his death. I would always dream that he would come back from the dead and that I wasn't sure what we had to do or how we could explain the situation. My dreams of Paul are not as regular as they once were, but when I need him, he will appear in my dreams which gives me great comfort.

After both my grandparents' deaths, I would often have dreams of them and we would be sitting around chatting and having afternoon tea. The dreams felt real and it was comforting knowing that they were still around watching over me. If my grandfather, Pa, would be in my dream, I would often say to him, 'What are you doing here, considering you are dead?'

Energy connection: Going home

The soul is our heart energy and the connection to our higher self. The mind or consciousness is the human connection and not the soul. Our souls are connected to our bodies by a silver cord, and once the body no longer exists or dies, the soul will detach the silver cord, leave the body and return home to heal and regroup. The soul may then decide to return back to earth to have another human experience.

Funerals

For years I have wondered, do those who have died visit their own funeral to see who attended and what it was like, having a bit of a sticky beak?

I have been to a few funerals over the years and have sensed the one who has died watching over their funeral. They tend to drop in have a look around and leave; I don't sense that they sit for the whole ceremony.

In early 2005, I attended a funeral for a work colleague who died tragically in a motor vehicle accident. He was in his mid-thirties and left behind a wife and two young children. The funeral was extremely sad, especially seeing his young family mourn. Whilst sitting in the church I could feel the heaviness around his coffin and this overwhelming sense of loss, and I felt as though his soul hadn't quite left his body, probably due to the tragic circumstances and him not knowing that he had actually died. In my mind, I kept saying to him, 'It is okay to leave your body and head home'.

I attended the funeral of a girlfriend's father-in-law in March 2017 in a small country town. During the service, all I could see was the father-in-law and mother-in-law, who had passed away a few years earlier, dancing in the middle of the church. It was lovely to watch as both souls were reunited and they were happy. After the service, we went outside and in the clear blue sky, this cloud appeared in the shape of angel wings. As I pointed it out to my girlfriend, we both experienced tingles throughout our bodies. The cloud proceeded towards their home as the hearse left the church. They were going home, together.

When my uncle died in February 2020 and I attended his funeral, I could sense him standing near the doors of the church and then he disappeared. When we were at the cemetery, I saw him again and as his coffin was being lowered, this beautiful light appeared in the sky. I watched him disappear and felt him leave, which was emotional but also beautiful to witness.

At my mother-in-law Val's funeral in March 2020, I didn't sense her there but Paul was at the church, floating around and trying to make me laugh because her funeral was at the same church as Paul's funeral had been. It brought back memories and I was overcome with sadness, so I could understand why Paul tried to make me laugh and keep it light. Even in death, Paul makes me laugh.

At Mum's funeral in late May 2020, I didn't sense her or see her, which was interesting. I am sure she would have had a peek to see who attended the funeral. I feel as though her soul checked out of her body a few days before her death. She seemed soulless and had probably had enough, packed her bag and there was no looking back.

Having all these personal experiences, I am convinced that as souls, we do come back to have a look at our funerals, purely as closure, ending the chapter of this life. As death is the finality of reality, the celebration of one's funeral is the closure of one's life.

Galaxy of Divinity (GOD)

The concept of God can be different for each person depending on their upbringing, beliefs, religious background, etc. My interpretation of 'God' is that it is an acronym for Galaxy of Divinity.

My concept of being with God or going home, which some may call 'heaven', is that as a soul, we are energy and one with the universe. We are energetically transporting throughout dimensions, having different experiences, evolving, lifting the energetic vibration of the soul.

I was discussing this concept with a friend who could relate, and they believed that 'God' meant Guardian of Destiny.

Messages from beyond

Messages from our loved ones can come in different forms, at different times and in different varieties. Our loved ones will communicate through all our senses, whether that's smell, feelings, hearing or vision. We can often see signs that remind us of our loved ones or indicate that they are trying to get in contact with us. These signs can be subtle or obvious.

Our loved ones will make an effort to try and get our attention by any means they can, and this is usually through electricity, or energy. After Paul's death, I would often hear the doorbell ring and then when I went to the door, there would be nobody there. The lamp in our lounge room would often flicker and when we still had the main landline phone connected, it would often ring and I would go to the phone, pick it up and there would be no one there, not even a dial tone, only silence. I am sure Paul was trying to call us from the other side.

Our dog would often sit and stare beyond me and then just bark at nothing, and I could sense Paul standing behind me.

When I was in Dublin in September 2019, I was fortunate to appear on the Ray D'Arcy Show to tell my story of travelling around the world with a cardboard cut-out of Paul. After my appearance with Ray I ventured back into the green room and one of the guests said, 'I just love your story'. As I sat down at the table where the group was sitting, the lady proceeded to tell me her story. Her name was Beth and she told me about a butterfly appearing out of nowhere in the middle of winter, where it was impossible for butterflies to be at that time of the year. The butterfly floated around her window for quite some time. Beth said she believed it was her mother letting her know she was happy and still watching over her.

Reincarnation: Multiple lifetimes

Have you ever visited a place you have never been to before and immediately felt as though you had? The surroundings feel familiar and you can walk through the streets and know that you have walked those streets before.

We have the opportunity to have multiple lifetime experiences in different places, cities and countries, and visiting those places will trigger memories. We can have flashbacks and the familiar feeling of being home.

I had that feeling when I visited London for the first time when I was on tour in 2017. I walked through the familiar streets of central London and immediately felt at home. I felt safe and could manoeuvre the streets without getting lost and found my way back to the hotel very easily. I have lived multiple lifetimes in England and can understand the feeling of being there before.

I had the same feeling, although more emotional and deeper, when I stepped off the bus at Stonehenge. As soon as I stepped onto the pathway, I was crying, absolutely sobbing, and I couldn't stop. I cannot explain the emotion that overcame me. I just couldn't put into words what I was experiencing, but I came up with the feeling of nothingness. It described exactly what the energy was about – it was silent, so quiet, so peaceful and tranquil as though time stood still. I had walked into another dimension; it was an amazing and life-changing experience.

By the time I stepped onto the bus that would take me up to the stones, I had composed myself and just stood there with the other passengers, with high expectations. When I arrived at the stones, I was not disappointed. The energy in this place was surreal, quiet, even though there were crowds around and the wind and rain were coming in sideways. I was in a totally different time and space. I had the feeling of coming home and felt sad but also happy. My heart was full with gratitude that I was able to come home again and know that I had walked here thousands of years ago as a druid. The flashbacks started and I could see my fellow druids gathering around the fire.

I walked further around the stones, trying to find a place that wasn't too windy or crowded, so I could take a photo. I found a somewhat less windy place, although people were everywhere and getting in my way, but I was able to take a few photos standing in front of Stonehenge.

My spidey senses were tingling as I continued to walk around the stones. Imagining back to when the druids walked this part of the earth, I had a strong sense of belonging, of being back home. My visit to Stonehenge was life-changing and I cannot describe the experience. It was breathtaking, amazing, nothingness and free.

When I returned to Stonehenge in September 2019, the same experience and feeling was there. I had the same emotional and energetic connection with Stonehenge and the tears fell freely. I will continue to return to Stonehenge, my home, as often as possible. It is such a magical, mystical, sacred space and a beautiful memory to be treasured.

In a conversation I had with Paul not long after he passed away, he was thinking of reincarnating and coming back to earth sooner. I reminded him that if he did come back earlier we may not meet again in my lifetime. I could hear him thinking and he said no, 'I won't come back but I will wait for you. I will be there to greet you when you eventually decide to come back home. So, when we do reunite again, we can plan our next journey together.'

A few months after that conversation we heard that our eldest son was going to become a father, and within twelve months of Paul's death, our grandson was born. As soon as I heard that we were expecting a grandchild, I looked up into the sky and said to Paul, 'I now understand that you had a small window of opportunity to make the decision to return back to Planet Earth.' I am extremely grateful that his soul decided to wait until my time has come to an end and I can return back home and reunite with my beautiful soul mate again. Although I truly believe that we met in a previous lifetime, our timing was not quite right.

Signs

Are you aware that the universe constantly gives us signs that relate to us? The issue may be that we are not aware or not looking for them.

Here is a good example of the universe letting me know about an experience I had in December 2015, when Paul and I were selling our speed boat. Two weeks after our boat was put up for sale, I was driving to work down the Calder Highway and a truck drove past with 'Stress Less Moves' written on it. I asked my guides, 'Has the boat been sold?' and the answer was yes.

Paul sent a text informing me that he had someone who was very interested in buying the boat and they were putting a deposit on it. The boat sold and moved out of the carport within two days of me seeing the truck.

The interesting thing about this story is that our boat was called 'Stressless'. How evident it is that a truck passed me letting me know that the boat was going to be sold! My lesson in this experience is to continue to look out for signs and confirm them with my team of spirit guides.

Can people who die communicate with the living? I continue to talk to Paul, and he still communicates with me through thoughts, feelings, smells and the signs of the Mini Cooper cars that I see. He also communicates through music. I often hear our songs, 'Unchained Melody' and 'Have I Told You Lately'. So, there must be something. I believe and know there is.

Because Mum passed away late in the evening, I organised for the funeral home to come and collect her body just after lunch on the following day. We were standing around chatting with Lawrence, the funeral director, and all of a sudden, the power went out. My brother-in-law, Warren, went to the switchboard to flick the power back on but it wouldn't come on. I was standing there getting full-body tingles, and I knew Mum was getting impatient and just wanted her body to leave the house. I said, 'Mum, we know you're there', and my sister yelled, 'Mum, this is not funny!' We did laugh though, and went around the house turning off all power switches. The power would not come back on until my sister went over to the new microwave and turned the switch off in the corner. The power came back on and we went into the lounge room to move Mum's body onto the gurney and take her to the funeral home to be placed in her coffin.

The next morning, I turned the power back on in the corner where the microwave was plugged in and didn't have any further problems.

Over the years, I have spoken to many people who have had similar experiences and have talked about lights flickering or someone knocking on the door or ringing the doorbell and no one is there. People have also received signs days before their loved one has died. These signs can be through various means, or can be just a heavy gut feeling of something foreboding.

Signs are on show for everyone to see, if only you just look. It doesn't have to be a loved one passing; there are many reasons to have an experience of witnessing signs.

Soul mates

The term soul mate is used to refer to a romantic or platonic partner with the perception of sole inclusivity and a lifelong bond. For some reason, humans believe that there is only one soul mate for them in any one lifetime. I am not sure where this belief or perception stemmed from, but my understanding is that we have multiple soul mates in any one lifetime. If we limit ourselves to believing we only have one soul mate, then we are limiting our outlook and setting ourselves up for failure and disappointment as we search for the true one. What happens if we search for our whole lifetimes seeking that true one, our soul mate, that we are supposed to meet and it doesn't happen? What if you were searching for this magical soul mate and missed the opportunity of actually meeting the right person for you in this lifetime?

We have multiple soul networks with family, friends, soul sisters and brothers, partnerships and relationships. These people come into our lives for a reason, whether it be short term, long term or eternity, as they assist with our life purpose to learn and grow. If we dismiss the opportunity of just meeting someone and release the perception of searching for the one, we may actually meet the person that we were supposed to meet in this lifetime.

I was very fortunate to meet my soul mate in this lifetime, even for a short time. My late husband and I met through work and just connected on so many levels; it was as if we had known each other for years. I remember that when we were first introduced the instant connection was electric, although we had to wait a few more years to move into a romantic partnership. Paul and I connected because we were meant to meet to complete our contract together. Although we spent thirty-two years together, we accomplished so much in that short time and helped each other grow. Paul's death provided me with an opportunity to grow exponentially, finding my passion for writing, becoming a published author and keynote speaker and expanding my spiritual journey.

Soul matrix

In one of my conversations with Paul after he had passed away, I asked if he had met up with David Bowie or Prince, because they had died around the same time that he did. Paul's response was 'don't be ridiculous', as those souls would return to their own frequency. He was not on the same frequency, so their meeting would be improbable. After our discussion, I had a more in-depth understanding of the soul's purpose and the term soul matrix was created.

As previously mentioned, the soul is electromagnetic energy. It vibrates at different frequencies and operates within a certain energetic range. The soul doesn't stay the same; each lifetime gives the soul opportunity to have different experiences to learn, expand and grow, increasing its vibrational frequency which is forever changing, as the purpose of the soul is to evolve.

This can explain why we meet certain people in our lives and connect, as we vibrate on equivalent or similar frequencies within that electromagnetic range. The soul attracts equivalent energetic frequencies, and when the soul returns home, it will automatically connect with similar energetic frequencies.

Paul went on to explain that when the soul returns home, it will automatically connect with loved ones but will eventually move on to other frequencies, depending on their experiences on earth and whether their soul has evolved by achieving their purpose in that lifetime.

To illustrate, imagine a year-seven and a year-twelve student in the educational system. These two students would not necessarily connect or be friends because of differences in their age, maturity and academic knowledge. They might be aware of or see each other in the school grounds or classes, but would not necessarily be friends or hang out together. This is similar to the soul matrix vibrational system – those souls that vibrate at a higher level don't necessarily connect with souls that haven't graduated to that level.

Spiritual team and contracts

When a soul decides to experience a journey on Planet Earth, it comes with a life plan, a contract and a team of helpers. When the soul makes the decision to reincarnate or have an experience on Planet Earth, prior to the actual birth process, the soul chooses the experience it wants to have based on the lessons it requires to evolve as a soul.

The soul makes the decision about what is required to fulfil and complete the lessons required. The soul chooses the form in which it will return to Planet Earth; for example, as a human being, male or female, an animal or whatever they would like to be, and once the decision has been made by the soul, a contract is arranged. This contract is based on an ethereal or spiritual level and not an actual legal document, and describes the plans in place to achieve that experience or lesson for a particular duration. The plan is comprehensive and as unique souls, we cannot do all this by ourselves. We surround ourselves with a team of helpers to move through our journey, to accomplish our plan and assist the soul on their earthly journey. Their purpose is to help us to accomplish our life purpose while we are on Planet Earth. They give us inspiration, insights and reassurance but they will never tell us what to do. These helpers are identified by many names, including angels, guides, and spiritual helpers.

The plan is flexible and can be changed to reflect the experience that the soul is seeking. The duration is somewhat flexible but only within a small window of opportunity. The soul makes these decisions well before coming on to Planet Earth, and they choose the team most suitable for the expedition as they require similar life skills and experiences that the soul wants to achieve. The team of helpers can also differ in size depending on the experience.

The more spiritual guidance they have, the more the soul will be interacting with other humans. Once all the plans and the contract are in place and the team is chosen, the soul will choose the parents that best suit their plans, so they can provide the grounding and teachings to start off life and the new soul's earthly experience.

During one of our conversations after Paul died, I asked why he chose the life he did. Why did he decide to leave so early in this lifetime? His response was that when he planned this life, he didn't realise how wonderful it was going to be, especially when he met me. He had already chosen the life he wanted to live and the experiences. Why he chose what he did, I have no idea. But I do know that if he hadn't experienced his journey and I hadn't been beside him, none of my books would have eventuated and I wouldn't be able to follow through with my purpose.

See, everything has a reason for happening. It may not make sense at the time, but eventually the penny will drop and you will get that lightbulb moment and say yes, now I understand.

When the soul has completed its contract and returned home, the soul may take time to readjust and heal from the experience on earth. The soul will also regroup and consult with their spiritual helpers about what was achieved and whether they were completely satisfied with their journey as planned.

I recall that not long after Paul passed, he was continuing to give me pictures or flashbacks of his time in hospital. I couldn't understand why and I didn't want to relive that time over and over again. When I asked him for the reason why he kept giving me those flashbacks, he explained that his soul was going through the healing process from his perspective and that he was experiencing healing from my perspective. I found it amazing that this beautiful soul was healing not only from his own experience but also from my journey that we shared together.

The sun as an energy source

Our universe is vast, and as humans we are unaware of how massive the universe actually is. As souls, we are able to play out in the universe, our home.

From the information I have been channelled, I know that the sun is our direct energy source, so no wonder we feel happy and fantastic on a bright sunny day, with the warmth from the sun giving us a huge energy boost and universal hug.

We can top up our vibrational energy through our crown and third eye chakras. Imagine light coming through the crown chakra and third eye, tapping into the light source to boost up energy to lift your vibration.

As the sun provides our energy, the moon energy is totally different and vibrates on a very subtle, secretive unknown energy that is softer and more feminine. We know that the energy of the moon is very mystical and taps into our creativity. The moon also affects our ocean tides and can play with our moods, especially around a full moon.

Tingles and vibrational energy

You will often hear people talk about tingles or shivers, especially if they are working in the spiritual field. Sometimes we might say that old expression of 'someone has walked over my grave', which is another form of chills. When connecting with spiritual guides or even coming into contact with a spiritual being, apparitions or ghosts, you may sometimes feel tingling or chills, or even feel your skin crawl or the hairs stand up on your arms. The reason for this is that energetically, humans vibrate at 4 kilowatts of energy, while spiritual beings vibrate at 4.5 kilowatts. This is why when connected, we feel the difference in energy by way of chills or tingles. It is a bit like walking on carpet and zapping someone else when we come into contact with them, purely because of the electricity built up.

I have found that the more I increase my energy frequency, the more intense the tingles become until they are full-body shivers.

Henry VIII

When I was travelling around Britain and Ireland in 2017 with a group of other tourists, I had some very weird and strange occurrences that are difficult to explain.

We had the opportunity to visit Windsor Castle, and our first stop was Queen Mary's dolls' house, which was amazing and not what I was expecting. This dolls' house was huge and had multiple rooms and miniature furniture. There was also a display of different dolls and their outfits and different types of other toys.

After wandering around the dolls' house, we proceeded towards the state apartments. When entering these rooms, I could feel different energy and it was changing from room to room. When I entered the king's bedroom, I felt as though someone was trying to stop me, like I was being blocked from entering. I was starting to feel dizzy and sick and was nearly knocked off my feet, which I knew wasn't me. Whoever the spirit was that was hanging around, they didn't want me there and they were making their presence felt. This was the case in many of the rooms that I entered, and I could feel the coolness in the air and the changing frequencies as I walked from one room to another. I am sure there were a few old kings still hanging around the palace that hadn't moved on.

After walking through many of the rooms, I felt a presence that seemed familiar and I asked who it was. The reply was Henry VIII. This was my first encounter with Henry but not my last.

I ran into Henry again when we toured Hampton Court Palace, and as I walked up to the front entrance, I felt him walking beside me. I laughed and asked Henry if he needed assistance in going back home, and he declined and said that he was having too much fun walking amongst the living and connecting with people like myself.

I came across Henry again when I was back in London in 2019 and visited the Tower of London. I was sitting quietly in the Chapel of St John. Henry appeared again and I was chatting with him and admonishing him for the cruel way he disposed of his wives, and how barbaric he was to have over 72,000 people executed. The thought that came to me was that this was what they did at that time, and the following popped into my head:

We cannot change the past
But we can change the future
By our actions in the now

I have had a few conversations with Henry since. I asked him if we had ever met, and he told me that we had and that I used to move in the same circles – I was in his court on numerous occasions. And according to a conversation I had with Paul, Henry and I knew each other when he ruled, and that we were both young and I flirted with the young Henry and had a liaison.

I am certainly thankful that Henry and I didn't go any further than a fling because I would not have wanted to be beheaded in the way that he executed two of his wives. When Henry visits, he tends to be the young and fun version, rather than the older, heavier Henry that is depicted.

Meant to be

On my travels, I get to meet some incredible people and visit some amazing places where we get to share our stories, and Dublin was no exception.

I was moving to my next accommodation, out near the airport for my last night in Ireland, after appearing on the Ray D'Arcy Show. I had booked a taxi to take me there. I was waiting at reception when a taxi pulled up and the driver came in to see who the fare was for. I approached him with my luggage and said, 'That would be me'.

As he put my luggage in the boot of the car, he started chatting away. Once we were both in the taxi, he told me that he had just dropped someone off at the hotel and was heading out when this job came in. He said, 'It must have been meant to be.' I left it at that, but towards the end of the journey, I knew that we were definitely meant to meet.

The taxi driver's name was Noel and he had this lovely broad Irish accent, complete with Irish profanities, and he was full of life and stories. We talked about the current issue of Brexit which was all over the media and had a huge impact on Ireland. Everyone had an opinion on Brexit and the UK leaving the European Union and Noel was no different. His attitude towards the UK was not pleasant by any means. After coming to the conclusion that Brexit would be a long, drawn-out affair, we moved on to other topics.

Noel eventually asked why I was visiting Ireland as he had picked up on my Australian accent. I told him I had some media commitments in Dublin, speaking about travelling around the world with a cardboard cut-out of my late husband Paul. He turned around and said, 'I know you, I heard about you on the radio yesterday. You were on the Ray D'Arcy TV show.' I confirmed that I was. He told me how brave and courageous I was and how he loved the idea.

Noel then told me the story of a lady who had hailed his taxi. When she got into the car, she asked about the white feather that was sitting on his dashboard and he told her the story behind it. She went on to tell him that she had recently lost her mother and prior to getting into his taxi, she had asked her mother to show her a sign that she was with her. The white feather was the sign, a promise prior to her death that every time she saw a white feather, she would know her mother was with her. The lady went on to tell Noel that it was amazing how many white feathers she does see out of the blue, and this was just another occasion and confirmation that her mother was close by. This brought her great comfort.

Noel then asked me whether I still talk to Paul and I said yes, all the time. He asked whether he talks back, and I said, 'Yes, of course. Most of the time.' I went on to tell Noel that my sign from Paul was the Mini Cooper motor vehicles and how amazing it is that I see them all the time, especially when I am travelling.

This is when Noel opened up and told me the story behind the white feather. His daughter committed suicide at the age of twelve due to being bullied at school, and her brother found her and had to cut her down and then tell his mother what had happened. Eight years later Noel was still grieving, upset and angry because of what happened. We both had tears in our eyes and I said, 'I am saddened to hear you lost your little girl in such a devastating way.' I asked him if he talks to her and he said yes, of course. I asked if she talks back and he said yes, sometimes. The white feather is a reminder that his daughter is an angel.

Noel then told me the story about his son losing his mobile phone at their property, which was on forty-five acres with knee-high grass. They had been searching for some time and Noel asked his son if he had rung it, and he said yes but the battery was now flat. Noel then asked him if he had asked his sister for help, and he said no. After walking around for some time, Noel called his son over to where he was standing and told him to look down. The phone was laying at Noel's feet, because he asked his daughter to help find the phone and she led him to exactly where it would be. I was getting full-body tingles. I said to Noel, 'How amazing. You just cannot make this stuff up', and he agreed.

We went on chatting some more, especially about people who don't know what to say in these situations and how people say 'I know how you are feeling'. He became very angry and said, 'No, unless you have walked a mile in my shoes, you have no idea how I am feeling'. And I totally agreed with him. We also went on to discuss all the special occasions and the anniversaries that they would miss. His daughter's anniversary was only a few weeks away, so the emotional build-up was evident. I also told Noel that Paul would miss out on walking our daughter down the aisle; she has three brothers to do that, but it wouldn't be the same. I told him I knew that Paul would definitely be there in spirit. To say that it was an extremely emotional moment would be an understatement.

I finally arrived at my hotel and Noel pulled my luggage from the boot. We stood in front of each other and then shared the biggest hug and wished each other well.

At that time, in that place, I was meant to be sitting in that taxi meeting Noel, and he the same. It was meant to be.

Medium work

As a trans medium, I have the opportunity to connect with souls that have had an earthly experience, which can span over multiple lifetimes. I am fortunate to still be able to connect with the souls of my late husband Paul and my mother Loryn, and I am privileged to be able to connect others with their loved ones who have passed and convey messages from beyond.

I am also able to assist lost souls and souls in confusion to connect with their spiritual helpers to return home, which is commonly called spiritual rescue work or trans healing.

Conversations with Paul

Since Paul's death, I have had numerous conversations with him. Some are insightful, as he has provided information about what it is like on the other side. Here are just two significant conversations that provide an amazing insight into the beyond and the endless love he has for me.

Walking Ollie around the block – 15 February 2017

> *I am very proud of you and you now need to live your life without me hanging around you.*
>
> *I am here for you always, I just had to disconnect energetically because we were both picking up each other's loss, more mine than yours. It doesn't mean I*

have completely left and let go. I will be here until you return and will be waiting for you.

I love you, my darling, always.

I know you need to move forward, so letting go energetically is the best way for you to do this. We are connected on many levels and this is the most connected and powerful. We have that connection, that soul connection, always.

Go have fun; you deserve it. You are an absolute saint and put up with so much shit when I was alive, and I am forever grateful to you for doing that for me. Now I can help you from the other side by making things happen for you. Protecting you and your reputation and ensuring you are safe and financially secure to live your purpose.

You have so much work to do and people to help. You are amazing and will be amazing.

I am here for you when you need my help, as it is my turn to help you. I won't get in the way and feel jealous with what will happen in the future, but know that we are always connected and I will be there for you when you come home. You will come home to me and I will be waiting for you with open arms and so much love you won't believe it.

You are a free soul and can love again, whoever you want. I have loved you for eternity and will continue, but whilst you are on earth you need someone to care for you and love you unconditionally, and you deserve that for however long you remain on earth.

You are free to love again and move on with your life. I am in the past and I am in your future but not in the now on Planet Earth.

I will always love you, always.

And then he was gone.

Encounter with Paul in the sauna – 26 June 2019

I was sitting in the sauna, relaxing and just enjoying the peace and solitude – plus, it was relaxing my tight muscles. Paul's voice came into my head. I could feel him there with me and we started chatting telepathically. It went something like this:

Paul told me that leaving his body and this life for the afterlife was an amazing experience and I should try it sometime! I laughed and said I do have a few more years to live, so I won't be trying it too soon. But it was very interesting to hear that the experience was amazing for him.

I asked Paul if he enjoyed travelling with me as a cardboard cut-out and he said yes, it was hilarious – especially when people gave us weird looks. I asked if my book,

#travellingwithcardboardPaul, would be successful, and he said it would because he was in the book. Again, I laughed.

We talked about my new love (if he ever turned up!). Paul said I will always find love. The man coming into my life is someone that I have met in a previous lifetime, someone who lost their wife tragically many years ago. The new man will look after me and I will help him find happiness and fun again.

We talked about Henry VIII and how we knew each other when he ruled. We were both young with the fun, young Henry.

Paul told me that he loved me and was glad that we could sit and talk as we were.

He told me that I would travel overseas with the book, and while I wouldn't be appearing on Ellen, there will be something bigger which will be a huge surprise. I mentioned how much fun it would be to meet Jimmy Fallon (we both watched his show every night it was on) and he said Jimmy would be aware of me.

We spoke about our love and connection. We are each other's true love and Paul will be there waiting for me when the time comes.

Paul came to me as the young Paul, the Paul I fell madly in love with from our first meeting. He spoke about family and how proud he is of Sarah and Matthew and each of their achievements in their careers. He told me that he spends a lot of time around Jordan, our grandson, and mentioned his ex-wife Pam and how he could spook her.

Paul said on numerous occasions how much we loved each other. He is often around me and mentioned the Mini Coopers as his sign to me so that I know he is around and think of him when I see one.

He has met up with family on the other side. I asked about Mum and he said she is fine, and will be okay; nothing will get her as she is tough and a survivor.

He reminded me of the scene from *Ghost* and our song, 'Unchained Melody'.

Then he was gone.

Lisa's story

I asked Lisa, the beautiful soul I met overseas in 2017, to put some words together about the loss of her husband, Tom, and anything spooky she had experienced. Here is Lisa's story.

A couple of days after Tom passed, Lisa had a very strange experience. She was in the dining room when she felt a presence, a strong breeze that passed by her. Lisa wanted to believe that Tom was there saying goodbye. This was the only encounter Lisa felt after Tom's death.

Ryan and Lisa picked out a beautiful pewter urn to keep Tom's ashes in after he passed away. They had it sealed, never thinking that it would need to be opened again. Tom's ashes had a permanent home for years on a memorial shelf built in Lisa's previous townhouse. In 2015, Lisa moved to a small apartment and gave away everything that was 'theirs', and started over with new furniture to have her own little 'bachelorette pad'. As strange as it may sound, Lisa put the urn into storage because she didn't want to bring any sorrow or negative vibes into the new apartment.

Lisa and Ryan booked a cruise to Hawaii in 2016. Lisa planned to meet Ryan in Seattle, where he lived, and then fly on to Honolulu together. Lisa thought of spreading Tom's ashes in Hawaii and needed the urn to be opened to retrieve some of Tom's ashes.

Lisa was handed Tom's ashes in a clear plastic bag and she packed him into her checked luggage. When Lisa arrived at the airport, her bag was five pounds over the limit. The airline agent suggested she could remove something or pay for excess luggage. Lisa removed Tom's ashes and put him in her carry-on luggage. That did the trick. It seems Tom didn't want to fly under the plane but beside Lisa.

It got weirder, though. When Lisa went through security, she told the Transportation Security Administration (TSA) about the remains and had the certificate of death for proof. They put a pair of scissors on the bottom of the container and the bag of ashes on top and sent it through the x-ray. Lisa asked why and they said they were looking to ensure there was no contraband inside. If they saw scissors, it was okay. Who would think to put something inside ashes? Lisa never expected anything like that.

Once Lisa arrived in Seattle, she and Ryan decided to spread Tom's ashes in a park near his house so that when he took his dogs there, he could be with his dad. They found a beautiful tree overlooking a lake and spread the ashes under the tree and spoke a few words and felt this was the right thing to do.

On reflection, they both thought it made more sense to have him close to one of them, instead of being in Hawaii. Lisa kept a small portion of Tom's ashes and spread them in the bushes under her apartment window and around a tree behind the apartment. That way, as long as she lived there, he was with her.

Lisa and I had the privilege of meeting on a twenty-day bus tour of England, Scotland, Ireland and Wales in October 2017. We commiserated with each other, having had very similar experiences of loss. Lisa had fun travelling with cardboard Paul; she said it was a novelty, to say the least. She noticed that it gave me a sense of relief having him close and sharing the different locations that we would have travelled together. Our friendship grew and we keep in touch to this day. Lisa is very excited about my accomplishments and thrilled to relive the experiences in the book #travellingwithcardboardpaul. She said that having been with me and then reading about it in the book was a hoot.

Weird stuff always happens

I will never forget the tragic circumstances of the eleventh of September 2001, when terrorists flew two aeroplanes into the twin towers of the World Trade Centre in New York. I remember that day like it was yesterday. I had been watching the news bulletin on television in our family room. I stood in shock like everyone else on that day, watching the planes fly directly into the buildings.

Whilst standing in front of the television, the temperature in the room dropped. The blinds started swaying in the breeze, and as I looked around to see what was going on, there stood a group of firemen in spirit. These firemen had been the first responders to the scene and had perished in the unfolding terrorist attack. I acknowledged them and felt so much sadness and confusion. They asked if they could watch the news with me and I said of course. As these men stood in my family room in spirit, I felt extremely honoured but also very emotional. They stood there for a while and then thanked me and vanished. I will never forget that experience. I knew they were heading back home. I wished them well and a safe journey with their guidance. And then I wept.

Final word

As an individual unique soul, seek to discover who you truly are. Seek your own truth and wisdom, and seek the information and knowledge that resonates with you. There is so much information available at your fingertips. Some information may be perfect for what you are seeking, and some not as useful. When you open your heart and follow your guidance, you will find exactly what suits your exact needs. And sometimes, when you are ready, the teacher or mentor will appear.

The fun and excitement is the journey of discovery and growth you will obtain in your soul's evolution.

Blessings, fellow soul searchers.

About the Author

Michelle Bourke is a storyteller who writes about true life – from losing her beloved husband, Paul, to cancer to recreating her life without him by her side. Michelle was born and raised in Melbourne and married her soul mate in 1991. They raised their two children in their home in Taylors Lakes.

Michelle has known from a young age that she had a special gift, being able to see spirits and having an inner understanding, being intuitive. Spending many years developing her gifts and gaining knowledge, she runs a series of personal and spiritual development talks and workshops, providing guidance to those seeking to develop their own true purpose.

Michelle a Trans-medium for over 30 years was able to use her spiritual gifts and inner knowing to assist her husband Paul on his final journey on earth after being diagnosed with a terminal illness in January 2016.

This spiritual belief and inner knowing became a great comfort when losing her soul mate and love of her life, supporting her during the grieving process.

After Paul's death in May 2016, Michelle wrote Conversations with Paul, a story about a journey of love, heartache, frustration and determination whilst facing a loved one's terminal illness.

Michelle has travelled around the world with a cardboard cut-out of Paul, keeping promises and writing her second book #travellingwithcardboardpaul sharing her stories of their amazing adventure.

Michelle is authentic, real and a born leader, empowering others by inspiring them with her determination to help others on their own true path.

In her third book, Michelle incorporates her experience with death and dying and beyond.

To connect with or learn more about Michelle, visit:

- www.beingconnected.com.au

- www.michellebourke.com.au

Other books by
Michelle Bourke

Notes :

www.ingramcontent.com/pod-product-compliance
Lightning Source LLC
Chambersburg PA
CBHW021154080526
44588CB00008B/335